BUILT FOR SUCCESS

THE STORY OF

Pixar

Published by Creative Paperbacks
P.O. Box 227, Mankato, Minnesota 56002
Creative Paperbacks is an imprint of The Creative Company
www.thecreativecompany.us

DESIGN BY **ZENO DESIGN**
PRODUCTION BY **CHELSEY LUTHER**
ART DIRECTION BY **CHRISTINE VANDERBEEK**
Printed in the United States of America

PHOTOGRAPHS BY Alamy (AF archive, Moviestore collection Ltd), Corbis (ALESSANDRO BIANCHI/Reuters, Owen Franken, Fred Prouser/Reuters, Louie Psihoyos, Roger Ressmeyer), Getty Images (Michael Kovac/FilmMagic, Paris Match, Justin Sullivan), Newscom (Disney Pixar/ZUMA PRESS, RICHARD KOCI HERNANDEZ/KRT3, Lisa Fierro iPhoto Inc., ROMAIN RAYNALDY/AFP/Getty Images, WALT DISNEY PRODUCTIONS/Album)

LIBRARY OF CONGRESS CATALOGING-IN-PUBLICATION DATA
Gilbert, Sara.
The story of Pixar / Sara Gilbert.
p. cm. — (Built for success)
Summary: A look at the origins, leaders, growth, and innovations of Pixar, the movie studio founded in 1986, which is one of the most successful producers of computer-animated films today.
Includes bibliographical references and index.
ISBN 978-1-60818-396-8 (hardcover)
ISBN 978-0-89812-983-0 (pbk)
1. Pixar (Firm)—Juvenile literature. 2. Animated films—United States—Juvenile literature. 3. Computer animation—United States—Juvenile literature. I. Title.

NC1766.U52P58347 2014
384'.806573—dc23 2013029615

CCSS: RI.5.1, 2, 3, 8; RH.6-8.4, 5, 6, 8

First Edition
9 8 7 6 5 4 3 2 1

BUILT FOR SUCCESS

THE STORY OF

Pixar

SARA GILBERT

The staff at Pixar was anxiously awaiting the release of the reviews for the company's first full-length feature film. Only a few employees had been lucky enough to attend one of the November 1995 premieres of *Toy Story*—and they knew that audiences had loved it so much that many adults had sobbed during the movie. When the *New York Times* was opened on the morning of the film's official release, the anxiety in the Pixar offices turned to delight. *Toy Story* was described as "a work of incredible cleverness," and its director, John Lasseter, was called "inspired." As similar reviews appeared in other newspapers and magazines, Pixar posted a short statement on its website: "Quite honestly, we're totally amazed by how much good press our little movie has gotten."

CHAPTER ONE

The Path to Pixar

In 1979, film producer George Lucas called computer scientist Ed Catmull and asked him to come to California to work for his company, Lucasfilm. Lucas had become famous after his 1977 film *Star Wars*, which was considered groundbreaking for its special effects, and was working on the sequel, *The Empire Strikes Back*.

He had learned of Catmull's design team and their developments at the Computer Graphics Laboratory at the New York Institute of Technology (NYIT), and Lucas wanted to harness such inventiveness to make digital technology that could be used in any stage of the filmmaking process, from editing and printing to creating computer graphics.

It was exactly the call Catmull had been waiting for. He and his coworker Alvy Ray Smith had been visiting movie studios in California every summer for at least three years, trying to sell **executives** on the idea of using computer graphics in their films. He accepted the job as head of Lucasfilm's new Computer Division and moved to San Anselmo, California, where his office was located in a small building above an antique shop. His hope was that, in addition to modernizing Lucas's process, he could demonstrate how computer technology could be used to generate films in their entirety.

Lucasfilm pioneered special effects and computer animation in movies such as *Star Wars*

Within a year, Catmull had recruited Smith and five other former coworkers—all designers and computer programmers—from the NYIT to join him at Lucasfilm. Then he found Loren Carpenter, a programmer from aircraft manufacturer Boeing, who had created a short animated film showing what it was like to fly over a mountain range, and brought him on board as well. And in 1983, Catmull hired John Lasseter, a former Walt Disney Company **animator** who was particularly interested in bringing inanimate objects to life with the help of computer programs.

Lasseter had actually just been fired from Disney. He had combined traditional animation with two-dimensional computer animation on a test **short** and wanted to use the technique on a feature film called *The Brave Little Toaster,* but he had stepped on a few toes while trying to convince his bosses at Disney to approve. When the project was rejected, Lasseter was let go. With time on his hands, he decided to attend a conference on computer graphics in Long Beach, California, where Catmull was speaking. Catmull had met Lasseter earlier that year and had been impressed by him—and now he was thrilled to bring him on to his team.

Catmull had to convince Lucas that Lasseter was a necessary addition, so he made up a title for him (Interface Designer) that no one knew what it meant. Lasseter's real assignment was to lead the animation process on a short computer-animated film called *The Adventures of André and Wally B,* which would demonstrate the work the Computer Division had been doing on computerized **rendering**, at the 1984 Special Interest Group on Graphics and Interactive Techniques (SIGGRAPH) conference. The experiment was also intended to show Lucas what the team and the technology they were developing were capable of accomplishing in terms of filmmaking.

Lucas was impressed but not for the reasons Catmull's team had hoped he would be. He thought the film itself was awful, with a thin storyline and primitive character design. "He couldn't make the leap from the crudeness of it then

Disney went on to make *The Brave Little Toaster* (1987) without John Lasseter's input

to what it could be," Smith said. "He took it literally for what it was and assumed that's all we could do." What Lucas found compelling, however, was the computer system that had been designed to make the film. That system, known internally as the Pixar Image Computer, was built to assemble the thousands of images that were used to create a final film; it was also used for touch-ups, color corrections, and rotating camera frames to the correct alignment. Lucas recognized that this technology could be valuable and decided to try to sell it, along with the Computer Division of his company, for $15 million.

That wasn't as easy as Lucas had thought it would be. None of the **venture capital** firms or **investment banks** approached as potential buyers was willing to take such a risk. A handful of printing companies, medical equipment manufacturers, and even automakers were interested in the technology—but none was willing to pay $15 million for it. Walt Disney Productions appeared to be considering an **acquisition**, but at the last minute, it backed away from a deal.

That left just one potential buyer: Steve Jobs, who had cofounded Apple Computer in 1976 but was pushed out of the company in the fall of 1985. Catmull had met with Jobs early on to discuss the opportunity. Although Jobs was intrigued by the technology and saw potential in the company, he wasn't willing to spend $15 million on it, either. In late 1985, however, he reached out to Lucasfilm once more and found out that the asking price was now negotiable. Lucas had grown weary of trying to sell the division and was ready to shut it down instead. Jobs offered $5 million for both the technology and the 44 employees who worked with it. That offer was accepted, and on February 3, 1986, Jobs became the majority owner of Pixar, Inc. In an article in *BusinessWeek*, he expressed his optimism about Pixar: "This whole thing has the same flavor as the personal computer industry in 1978," Jobs said.

> *"Pixar's seen by a lot of folks as an overnight success, but if you really look closely, most overnight successes took a long time."*
>
> STEVE JOBS

Introduced in the 1970s, the Apple II was one of the first successful models of personal computers

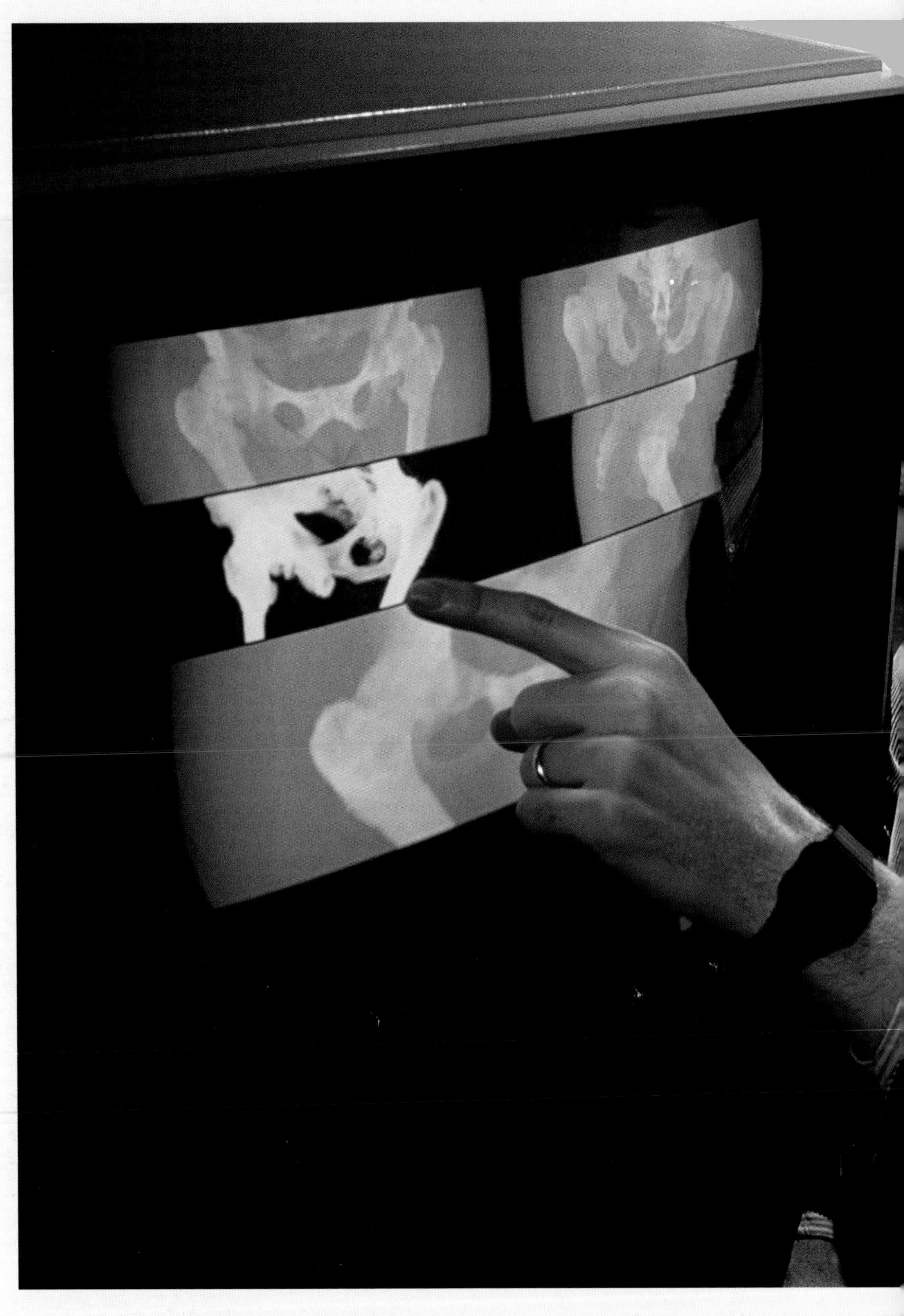

Ed Catmull with a Pixar monitor, 1985

MAKING UP A NAME

Pixar the company was named for Pixar the computer—and the computer's name was completely made up according to the whims of the people who had built it. In 1981, four of the men who had been working on a specialized machine that could facilitate computer animation went out for burgers. They were determined to agree upon a name for the computer before dinner ended. The first suggestion, "Picture Maker," was quickly dismissed. Using the word "laser" in the name also met with mixed reviews. But when Alvy Ray Smith, the director of computer graphics research, suggested making up a word that would mean "to make pictures," the idea stuck. His initial idea was "Pixer," but the rest of the team liked a variation with an "a" in place of the "e": Pixar. The Pixar Image Computer was born and became the ancestor of the company that would bear its name.

CHAPTER TWO

On the Jobs

Steve Jobs had purchased Pixar as a hardware company—a manufacturer of computer equipment—not as an animation company. His priority was to sell the Pixar Image Computers, and he was pleased when the company received orders for a number of the $125,000 machines from equipment and electronics manufacturing companies such as Philips, Sperry Corporation, and Symbolics as well as from several major universities.

Although Jobs didn't consider computer-animated films to be a source of **revenue** for the company, Catmull and Smith—now the company's chief technology officer and vice president respectively—justified maintaining a small animation department, consisting mainly of Lasseter, as a means of demonstrating what the company was capable of creating. Lasseter's next task was to make a short film to show at SIGGRAPH in 1986. His film, *Luxo Jr.*, in which two bendable desk lamps—one a parent, the other a child—played catch with a ball, received rave reviews at the conference.

Luxo Jr. broke new ground in terms of the realistic portrayal of inanimate objects,

The *Luxo Jr.* lamp and ball became permanent symbols of Pixar as a company

but it was the emotional realism of those characters that most impressed the audience. Lasseter was surprised when one person approached him afterwards with what he thought would be a technical question. Instead, the viewer asked, "Was the big lamp the mother or the father?" To Lasseter, that was proof that he had succeeded in making his characters believable, with humanlike emotional qualities.

As Lasseter was working on *Luxo Jr.*, his colleagues at Pixar were negotiating the final details of a deal with Disney to provide a **software** system called the Computer Animation Production System (CAPS) to the company. The system scanned the pencil drawings that Disney artists had created, colored them in, placed them onto scanned backgrounds, and recorded them on film. Disney tested CAPS on the final scene of the 1989 movie *The Little Mermaid*—where King Triton waves goodbye to his now-human daughter Ariel—and was so impressed with the results that the company immediately decided to use CAPS for all its animated feature films.

Disney became Pixar's largest customer, purchasing dozens of Pixar Image Computers on which to run the CAPS software. But that wasn't enough to help the young company turn its first **profit**. In fact, apart from Disney, sales had slowed considerably. Even a second smaller version of the computer, with fewer capabilities and a much lower price tag of just $29,500, didn't achieve the expected sales results. One of the software **engineers** at Pixar had an idea for another direction to pursue: a program for three-dimensional rendering, designed to create **photorealistic** computer graphics.

Jobs had high hopes for the new program, which came to be known as RenderMan. He thought that three-dimensional rendering had the potential to become almost as common as **desktop publishing** software and that it would be used in marketing materials and business communications for a wide range of customers. It turned out, however, that although RenderMan was well received by the computer animation community and movie studios producing special effects, the concept never caught on with a broader audience.

Catmull and the rest of the Pixar staff could tell that Jobs was growing

The Little Mermaid ushered in an era of acclaimed Disney films with a new style of animation

increasingly frustrated with Pixar's inability to turn a profit. In 1988, new chief executive officer (CEO) Chuck Kolstad brought together a core group of people to discuss ways in which the company could make money and further its moviemaking plans. The group concluded that using the talents of the animation team to create television commercials would help accomplish both goals.

Lasseter, whose movie *Tin Toy* had won the Academy Award for Best Animated Short Film in 1988, was excited about the opportunity. As contracts came in to create commercials for products such as Listerine, Trident gum, and Volkswagen in 1990, he was able to hire two new animators to help handle the workload. In 1991, Pixar produced 15 commercial spots, bringing in more than $2 million for the company.

The advertising work helped establish credibility for Pixar's animation staff and gave the company a chance to train new talent for the films they hoped to make someday. It was not enough, however, to solve Pixar's financial woes—and Jobs's patience was almost gone. In 1990, he had agreed to stop making the Pixar Image Computer and to sell the company's hardware division in order to focus on commercials and software development. But that year, Pixar lost more than $8.3 million and struggled to pay its bills on time.

Jobs put Pixar on notice by taking back the shares of ownership that employees had been allowed to purchase when he bought the company, becoming its sole owner—which meant that he could shut it down if he wanted to. In March 1991, he also laid off almost half of the company's employees—including Kolstad—keeping only those whose jobs were directly related to either the continued development of the RenderMan software or the creation of commercials.

Many outsiders were surprised that Jobs kept Pixar alive at all—and a few insiders were as well. "It wasn't really working," Alvy Ray Smith said. "We should have failed. But it seemed to me that Steve just would not suffer a defeat. He couldn't sustain it."

"Animation is the one type of movie that really does play for the entire audience. Our challenge is to make stories that connect for kids and adults."

JOHN LASSETER

Before *Toy Story*'s groundbreaking success, the future of Pixar executives and animators was uncertain

DON'T
STALK

MONSTER MIX-UP

When Lori Madrid saw a trailer for Pixar's *Monsters, Inc.* in September 2001, she was unhappy. The plot seemed similar to a story she had written several years earlier. She assumed that a publishing company she had submitted the story to had shared it with Pixar. Madrid filed a **lawsuit** against the publisher, Pixar, and Disney. The first hearing took place on November 1, 2001—one day before the scheduled release of *Monsters, Inc.* The judge allowed the movie to open as planned but didn't issue a ruling on the case until June 26, 2002, when he said that the ideas in the movie and the story were too universal to have been copied. "All of these ideas are standard and indispensable with these characters, and with children's stories in general," he wrote. "To say that such things may be protected by copyright laws would certainly be chilling to the free flow of children's stories."

CHAPTER THREE

The Disney Connection

A glimmer of hope for Pixar's future presented itself in July 1991, when the company signed a long-awaited contract with Disney to produce a full-length feature film together. Although the contract was far more favorable to Disney than to Pixar, it was exactly what Catmull and his team had been working toward for more than 10 years.

Lasseter began working on the **script** for a film he was calling *Toy Story*, but the Pixar team continued making commercials as if the Disney contract didn't exist. "There was no guarantee that Disney would stick through the whole process," said Ralph Guggenheim, then Pixar's vice president of feature animation. "They could bail out at any time."

There were times during the four years it took to complete *Toy Story* that Disney's backing seemed tenuous. The storyline and main characters were questioned; at one point, Disney even brought in outside **screenwriters** to rework the script. Even after the script was approved in January 1993, problems arose in November that required another rewrite. Finally, in April 1994, production began.

Throughout that span of time, Pixar was spending more money on *Toy Story* than it was bringing in, either from the Disney contract or the commercials it continued

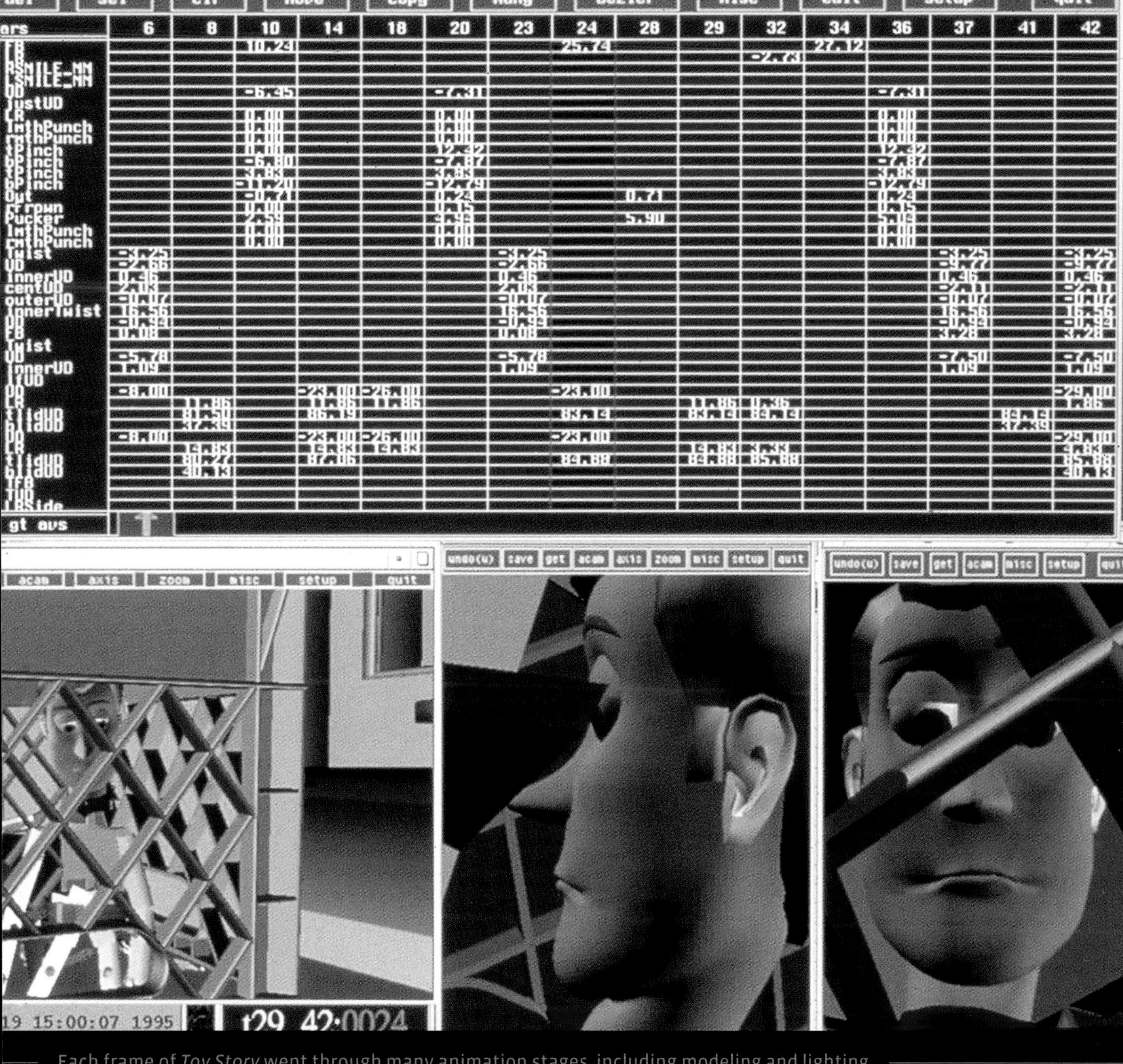

Each frame of *Toy Story* went through many animation stages, including modeling and lighting

to make. By that point, Jobs had invested almost $50 million in the company and was ready to cut his losses. He unsuccessfully tried to sell parts of Pixar to a number of other companies, including Hallmark. In the fall of 1994, he came close to a deal with software-maker Microsoft, but at the last minute he decided not to sell. Instead, he agreed to give Microsoft the use of several of Pixar's **patents** for a one-time fee of $6.5 million.

By then, Jobs had begun to see *Toy Story* as a turning point for Pixar. He was so sure of its success that he decided to take the company public, selling shares of ownership to the general public, after the movie's release. Although he was advised by lawyers and financial advisers not to move ahead with that plan as long as Pixar still wasn't profitable, Jobs was determined to see it happen.

When *Toy Story* opened in November 1995, Jobs's optimism was rewarded. In its first 12 days in theaters, it earned $64.7 million. Pixar's **initial public offering** was held just a week later, on November 29. The shares sold quickly—and for a much higher price than had been expected. By the end of the day, the sale had raised $132 million for Pixar, making Jobs, who owned 80 percent of the company, as well as select Pixar employees such as Lasseter and Catmull, immediately wealthy.

The success of *Toy Story*, which made almost $362 million at the box office worldwide and became the highest-grossing film of the year, went well beyond the money. In 1996, Lasseter was honored with a Special Achievement Academy Award from the Academy of Motion Picture Arts and Sciences for "inspired leadership of the Pixar *Toy Story* team, resulting in the first feature-length computer-animated film." Catmull, Smith, and two other members of the Pixar team also received an Academy Award for their pioneering role in digital image composition.

Such awards brought immediate recognition and prestige to the Pixar brand. Combined with the cash infusion of the public offering, Pixar found itself in a position to negotiate a new deal with Disney. A second movie—*A Bug's*

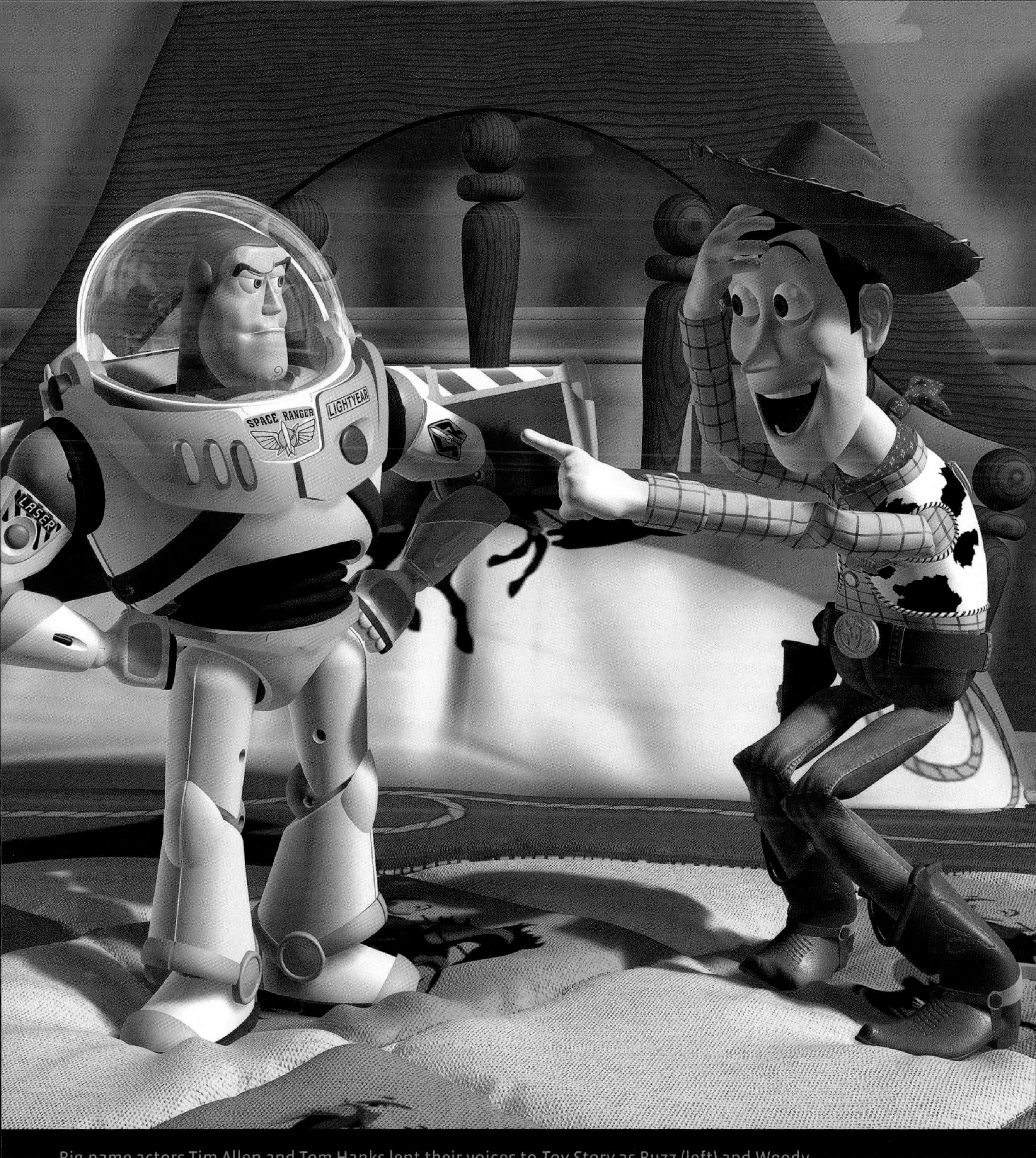

Big-name actors Tim Allen and Tom Hanks lent their voices to *Toy Story* as Buzz (left) and Woody

Life—was already in the works when, in 1997, a new contract that called for the two companies to collaborate on 5 films over a 10-year period was completed. This contract was far more balanced than the first, splitting both production costs and box-office profits evenly between the two companies. Under the new terms, Pixar was also given equal billing to Disney on each film and its associated advertising.

Not long after successfully renegotiating the contract with Disney, Jobs found himself celebrating another business victory—this time related to Apple instead of Pixar. He had returned to the company as an adviser in 1996, but in September 1997, he was asked to serve as its CEO. Jobs's staff at Pixar was happy for him and even a little relieved that his attention would be refocused on Apple. "There was a little bit of tension because he wanted to give Pixar more than Pixar actually wanted," said Pamela Kerwin, a Pixar marketing executive. "When he went back to Apple, it was great because that could really absorb his passion."

The distraction came at an unfortunate time, however. As *A Bug's Life* neared its November 1998 release, Pixar was engaged in a battle with former Disney executive and Pixar supporter Jeffrey Katzenberg and his new company, DreamWorks Animation. Katzenberg, who had known about the plans for *A Bug's Life* since 1995, announced that DreamWorks' first animated feature would be released in October 1998. It was called *Antz* and seemed suspiciously similar to the story of *A Bug's Life*.

Lasseter in particular was hurt that Katzenberg had betrayed him, but he publicly dismissed *Antz* as an inferior film. "It's sad, because they clearly stole the idea from us. But we haven't worried about that too much. We've put it behind us," he said. Lasseter was right not to worry; *A Bug's Life* made more than $358 million worldwide in its first year—twice as much as *Antz*.

> *"Most Pixar films are better than most live-action films."*
>
> FILM CRITIC WESLEY MORRIS

Despite early challenges, owner Steve Jobs was confident in Pixar's potential for success

BUILT FOR SUCCESS
PAGE 28

SUCCESS WITH SEQUELS

Disney was so pleased with the success of Pixar's *Toy Story* that it quickly began planning for its sequel. Disney's plan was to release *Toy Story 2* on video, rather than in the theater—a plan that had worked well for it in the past. But when Disney executives saw the early storyline for *Toy Story 2*, they realized that it was just as original and creative as the first—and that it might do almost as well at the box office, too. They were wrong: it did even better than *Toy Story* had. "*Toy Story 2* does what few sequels ever do," a review in *The Hollywood Reporter* said. "[It] delves deeper into the characters while retaining the fun spirit of the original film." Pixar's success with sequels continued with *Toy Story 3*, which was even more popular, and made even more money, than either of the first two.

CHAPTER FOUR

The Pixar Touch

In November 1999, Disney and Pixar released *Toy Story 2*. The sequel to their first joint venture was even more successful than the original film; it broke box-office records on its opening weekend in the United States, United Kingdom, and Japan, and was just behind *The Lion King* as the highest-grossing animated film of all time. It also solidified Pixar's reputation for producing top-notch movies.

With more of those movies in the works—each one taking four or more years to get from original concept to release date—and more than one usually in progress at any given time, Pixar was growing so large that the company had to find a new space for its 500 employees. Jobs found the company's new location in the small town of Emeryville, California: the 16-acre site of a former Del Monte fruit cannery, where Pixar built an enormous, 218,000-square-foot building in 2000.

In the new office, employees expressed themselves by decorating their workspaces in different themes (one employee's cubicle was designed as a tiki hut). Their creativity was also at work on a pair of new movies—*Monsters, Inc.*, which was released in November 2001, and *Finding Nemo*, which came out in May 2003—that

Pixar employees work at the Pixar Animation Studios campus in Emeryville, California.

would further prove that the Pixar touch seemed to turn any film into box-office gold.

Monsters, Inc. set a record for animated movies by making more than $100 million in its first 9 days and surpassed *Toy Story 2* to become the second-highest-grossing film of all time. *Finding Nemo* did even better, dethroning Disney's *The Lion King* as the top-grossing animated film of all time and winning the Academy Award for Best Animated Feature. The undeniable successes enjoyed by all five of the full-length films Pixar had produced led the *Los Angeles Times* to label Pixar "the most reliable creative force in Hollywood."

In 2004, *The Incredibles* earned the company its second consecutive Academy Award for Best Animated Feature. It also broke new ground for Pixar in that it showcased a human (or, super-human) cast, and it was the first to be directed by someone who hadn't risen through Pixar's internal ranks. Lasseter had directed the first three releases himself; Pete Docter and Andrew Stanton, the respective directors of *Monsters, Inc.* and *Finding Nemo*, had both been animators with the company for years before directing a film. But when Brad Bird came to Lasseter with his idea about a family of superheroes trying to make a new life as average Americans, Lasseter quickly invited the young director into the fold.

The Incredibles presented new technical challenges for Pixar; making human figures appear realistic was more difficult than working with fish or furry monsters. Perfecting the skin and hair was particularly trying for the animation team. Bird was so relentless in his requests for special effects and reworked scenes that he started getting what he called "the Pixar glaze" from the technical staff when he pushed for innovative ideas. But the attention to detail paid off: *The Incredibles* broke all of Pixar's previous opening-weekend records and earned high praise from critics as well.

Such success led to some contentious conversations between Steve Jobs and Michael Eisner, the CEO of the Walt Disney Company. The relationship between the two men, and the partnership between the two companies, had been rocky

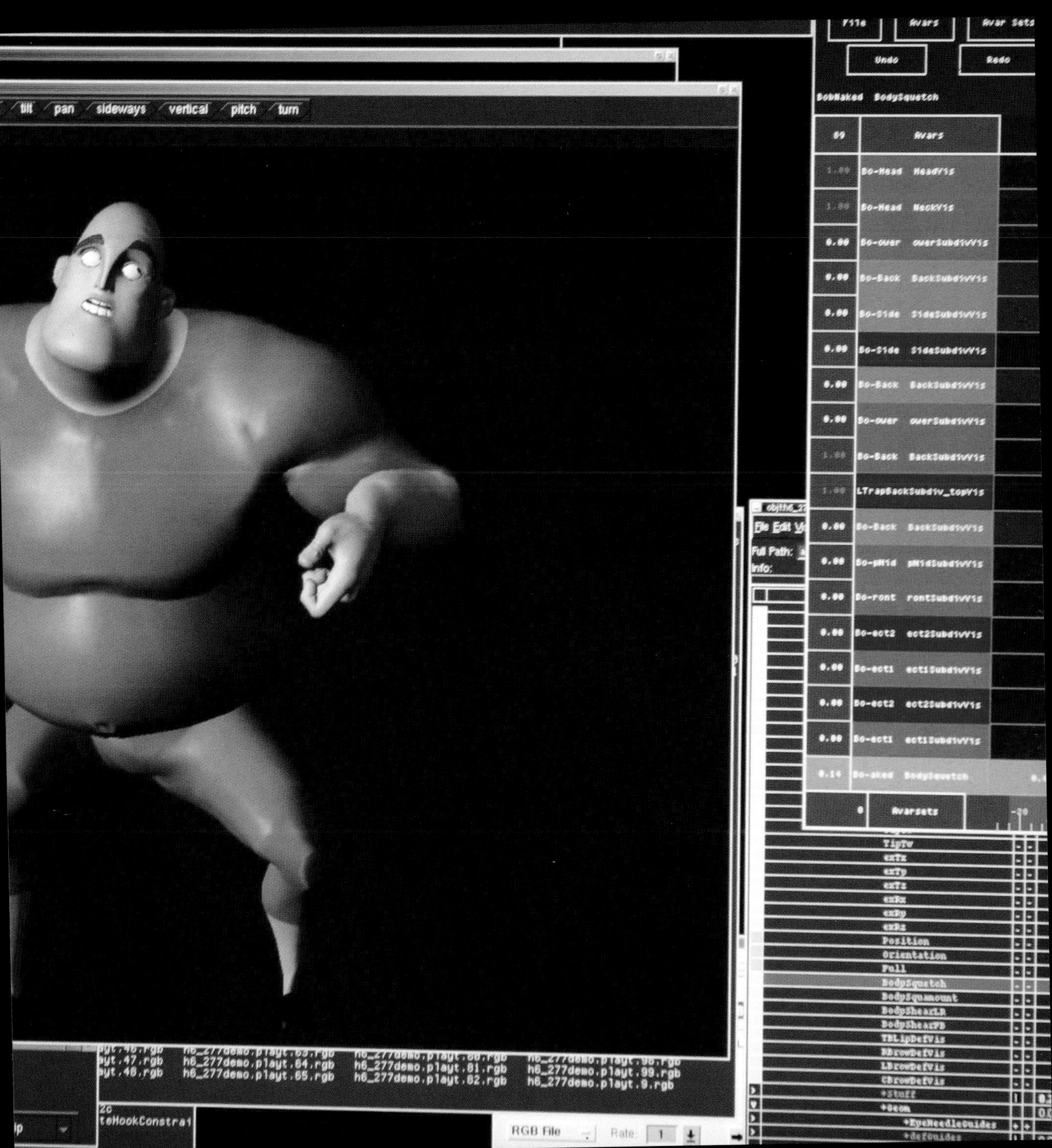

Pixar created new animation techniques for the human characters in 2004's *The Incredibles*

since Eisner had refused to include sequels—including *Toy Story 2*—among the five films Pixar had committed to make with Disney in 1997. Eisner further infuriated Jobs by making negative comments about Apple during a 2002 congressional hearing about **piracy** of digital films. Jobs vented his anger to Roy Disney, the chairman of Disney Feature Animation, telling him that Pixar was not likely to continue its relationship with Disney. "I'll never make a deal as long as Eisner is there," Jobs said.

The terms of a new deal that Jobs brought to Eisner in the spring of 2003 were so one-sided that it looked as though he was trying to make sure a deal didn't happen. His proposal did not include co-ownership of Pixar's films, as the previous agreement did. It also didn't split profits between the two companies; instead, Disney would receive only a distribution fee of 7.5 percent of the revenues. Eisner was neither impressed nor inclined to concede to Jobs's demands. After 10 months of waiting to resolve the situation, Jobs abruptly announced on January 29, 2004, that he was suspending negotiations and ending Pixar's relationship with Disney.

Jobs had other options—he had already been meeting with executives from other potential distribution partners, including Sony Pictures Entertainment. His company had no **debt**, was flush with cash, and was riding a wave of successful movies. Disney, on the other hand, was experiencing internal power struggles that left it unstable. It was also saddled with a string of lackluster movies that hadn't performed up to expectation. Even so, Eisner put a positive spin on the Pixar move, praising both Jobs and Lasseter for their leadership and creativity as he acknowledged the end of the partnership: "Although we would have enjoyed continuing our successful collaboration under mutually acceptable terms, Pixar understandably has chosen to go its own way to grow as an independent company."

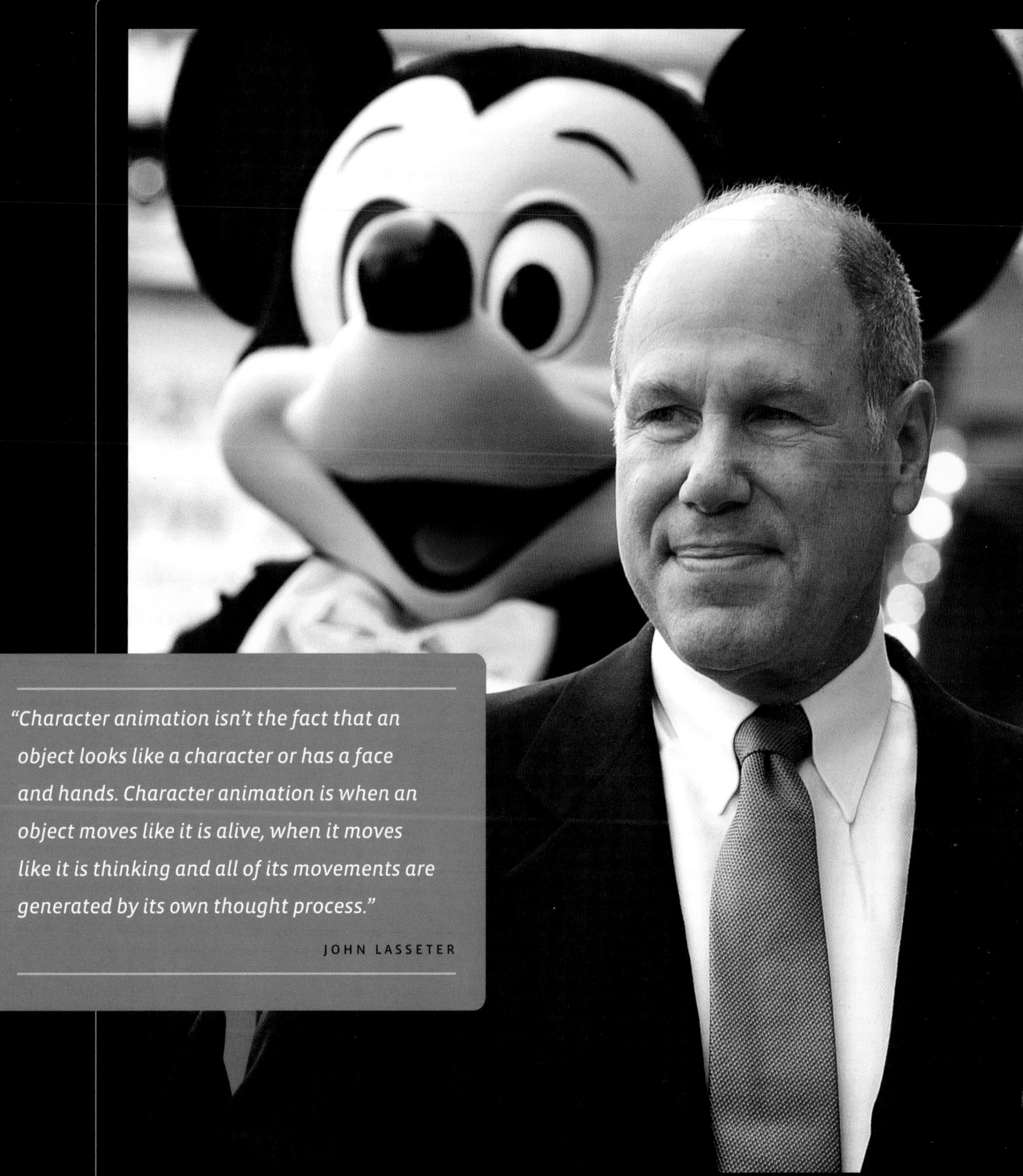

"Character animation isn't the fact that an object looks like a character or has a face and hands. Character animation is when an object moves like it is alive, when it moves like it is thinking and all of its movements are generated by its own thought process."

JOHN LASSETER

Conflict between Disney CEO Michael Eisner and Pixar largely stemmed from contract negotiations

AND THE AWARD GOES TO ...

By the end of 2012, Pixar had re-leased a total of 13 full-length feature films and at least 25 short films. Most of them had been nominated for at least one award, and many received multiple nominations from a number of different organizations—from the Academy of Motion Picture Arts and Sciences to Nickelodeon's Kids' Choice Awards and the MTV Movie Awards. Pixar films—and the people associated with them—have been nominated for more than 245 awards in all—and they've gone on to win more than 200 of those, including 6 Oscars for Best Animated Feature Film and 1 for both Best Original Song and Best Original Score. Two Pixar films—*Up* and *Toy Story 3*—have also been nominated for the Best Picture Academy Award. Only one of Pixar's full-length feature films—*Cars 2*—received no Oscar nominations. The most honored, as of 2013, was *WALL-E*, which was nominated for six awards.

CHAPTER FIVE

The New Deal

Pixar didn't stay independent for long. By the end of 2004, an embattled Eisner announced that he would be retiring in 2005, and his successor, Bob Iger, was eager to patch up the company's relationship with Jobs and, eventually, Pixar. His first step, however, was to partner with Jobs and Apple to provide access to Disney Channel television shows on the iTunes online music and video store in October 2005.

Iger's hope was that that deal—which took less than a week to finalize—would pave the path to a new relationship with Pixar as well.

The form of that new relationship occurred to Iger while he was watching a parade during the opening of Hong Kong Disneyland in September 2005. He noticed that all the newest characters in the parade were from Pixar films: Woody and Buzz Lightyear from *Toy Story*, for example, and Mike and Sulley from *Monsters, Inc.* He realized that Pixar was doing a far better job at creating animated films than Disney was, so he suggested to the Disney **board of directors** that they consider buying Pixar.

As Disney CEO, Bob Iger oversaw acquisitions of Pixar, Marvel Entertainment, and Lucasfilm

With the board's approval, Iger approached Jobs with the idea. Jobs was interested enough that he asked Catmull and Lasseter to join the discussion. But the conversations at that point weren't about price; Catmull and Lasseter were much more interested in how the two distinct animation studios would work together and how Pixar's creative culture would be maintained after an acquisition. Only after that point had been satisfactorily settled did they begin to discuss the dollars involved.

On January 24, 2006, Iger announced that Disney would purchase Pixar through an exchange of **stock** worth approximately $7.4 billion. Disney's animation studio in Burbank would remain there, and Pixar's staff would continue to work out of its site in Emeryville. Catmull was named president of the combined organizations, and Lasseter became the chief creative officer of both as well. Jobs, meanwhile, became a member of Disney's board of directors and the largest individual **shareholder** in the company. "Now," Jobs said as the deal was announced, "everyone can focus on what is most important: creating innovative stories, characters, and films that delight millions of people around the world."

Oddly, the first Pixar film released after the new Disney deal was also its first to perform below expectations. Although it won the Academy Award for Best Animated Feature and was the second-highest-grossing film of 2006, *Cars* made less money at the box office than any Pixar movie since *A Bug's Life*. It was also Pixar's first film to receive negative reviews in the press: "Pixar finally rolled out a clunker," a critic for *The Philadelphia Inquirer* wrote, while a reviewer for the *San Jose Mercury News* said it was "the first Pixar movie with which I've ever found myself getting bored."

Pixar celebrated its 20th anniversary in 2006 with far more **competition** than had existed when it started. Although the growth of computer animation companies was evidence that the vision of Pixar's founders had come to fruition, it also meant that families had more animated options at theaters than ever before. In 2006 alone, at least seven companies released computer-animated

Pixar created rookie race car Lightning McQueen (left) and tow-truck pal Mater for 2006's *Cars*

movies, from Animal Logic's *Happy Feet* to DreamWorks' *Over the Hedge*.

Pixar, however, still set the standard. It followed the disappointing performance of *Cars* with a series of releases that were not only financially successful but also critically acclaimed: *Ratatouille* in 2007, *WALL-E* in 2008, and *Up* in 2009. Each won an Oscar for Best Animated Feature, and *Up* was even nominated for the coveted Best Picture award—the first animated movie to earn such a nomination since Disney's *Beauty and the Beast* in 1991.

In 2010, Pixar enjoyed its biggest success to date with *Toy Story 3*, which made more than $1 billion on its way to becoming the highest-grossing animated movie of all time. It was nominated for five Academy Awards and won two of them—Best Animated Feature Film and Best Original Song. *Toy Story 3* was the last Pixar movie that Jobs was able to watch. On October 5, 2011, Jobs died at his California home after a long battle with cancer. Pixar honored his importance to the company by naming the main building on its Emeryville campus after him and by mentioning him in the closing **credits** of *Brave*, which was released in June 2012.

Thanks to Jobs's staunch support of its vision and his willingness to battle for its worth, Pixar was positioned to continue on without him. As part of the Walt Disney Company, Pixar had the financial stability it needed to continue making innovative and creative films that pushed the boundaries of computer animation. Among the movies in the works as of 2014 were a journey into the human mind; a celebration of the Mexican holiday *Dia de los Muertos*, or "Day of the Dead"; and a sequel to *Finding Nemo*.

If Pixar's track record is any indication, moviegoers can certainly expect to be entertained far into the future. Since its founding, the company has held true to its vision of using technology to make movies that tell great stories, and it likely will continue to do so to infinity—and beyond.

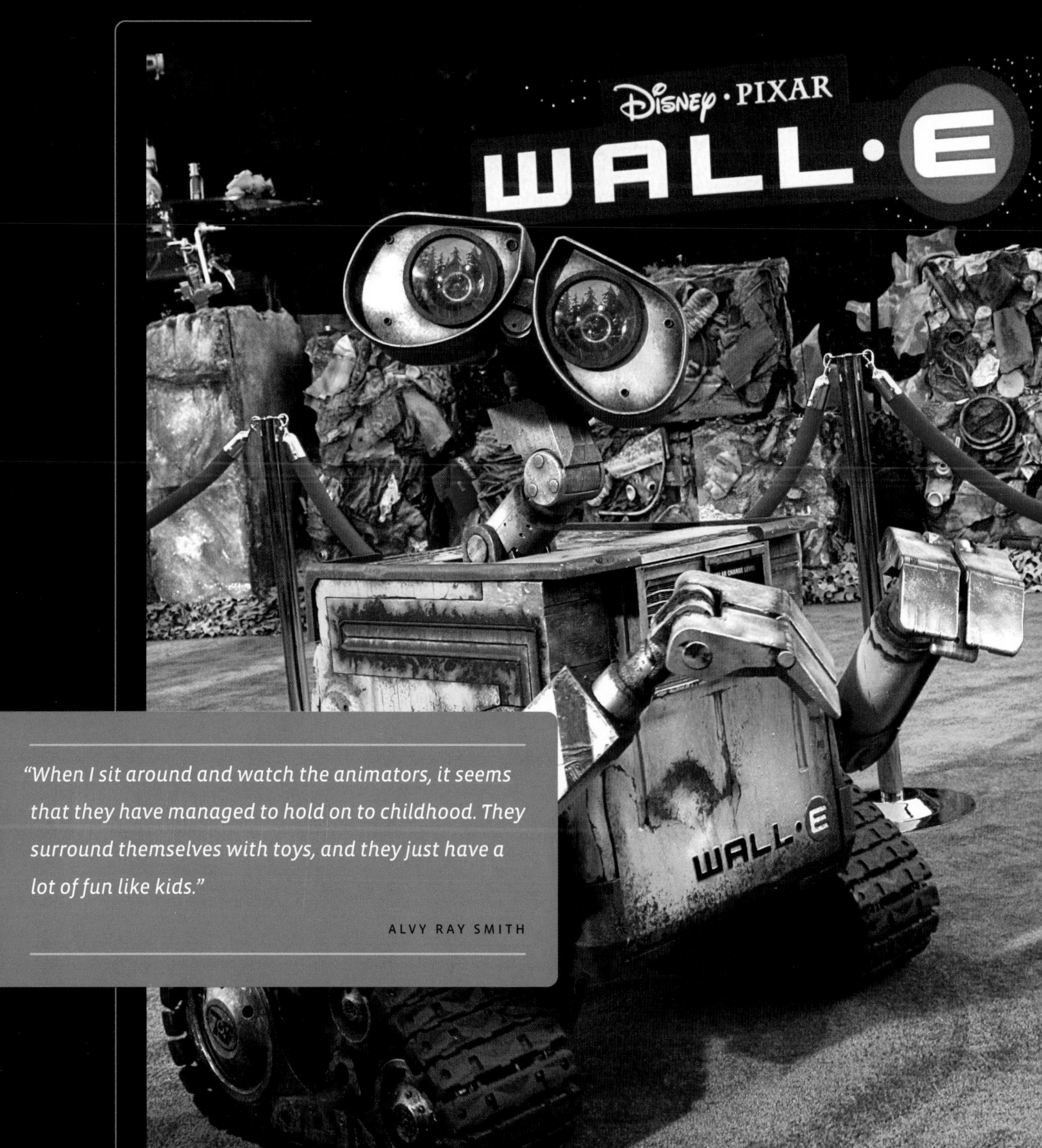

> *"When I sit around and watch the animators, it seems that they have managed to hold on to childhood. They surround themselves with toys, and they just have a lot of fun like kids."*
>
> ALVY RAY SMITH

WALL-E's robotic characters communicated through movements and sounds rather than dialog

NEW
WORLD
NEW WORLD
TO BE
DISCOVERED
IN
1492